HOMELESS
GOD BLESS

HOME LESS GOD BLESS

POEMS

David B Churchill

HOMELESS GOD BLESS

Cover art: *Gray and Gold*, 1942. John Rogers Cox (American, 1915-1990). The Cleveland Museum of Art, Mr. and Mrs. William H. Marlatt Fund. Courtesy of The Cleveland Museum of Art.

Book layout by Barbara Shaw

ISBN 978-0-975395-5-1

First Edition

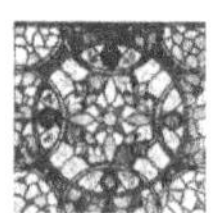

Published by:
Pony One Dog Press
Suite 113
1613 Harvard Street, NW
Washington, DC 20009

I went out to wait for you.
I found a corner to stand on.
My hair grew long.
I began to receive offerings . .

CONTENTS

HOMELESS
GOD
BLESS

Invocation

You never learned my name.
You may not think I had one—
or if you had asked,
I could even have told you.
But one day you walked past
where I sat in my silence,
considering the world,
and you looked in my face.
You saw a tree with the bark
stripped off, eyelids like moss
on a cliff, and a mouth—
you saw a mouth with no teeth,
a mouth like a footprint
in mud beside a lake.
Call me Homeless-God-Bless.
Even you may have walked on my face.

House of Clouds

August 2018, Washington DC

The house of clouds is tall—
how tall we wouldn't
know but for the
thousand-floor
column-forms
on wheels of air,
with room to spare.

It is the one thing
that doesn't shut us out—
because we're
already in it,
though we can never
walk its polished
halls nor climb its stairs.

On any planet will
this house be blue
and full of turbaned forms?
or in this life only
are we blessed
to know its all is edged
with airy gold?

Homeless Camp is Gone

All day winter
sent its rear-guard winds
to blast
the beginning of its end,
and blew a homeless tent
apart,

so when I passed,
I saw its constituent
parts torn
into flags of disrepair—
except for a fence
of rubbish

neatly built
about its periphery,
was not disturbed—
This the wind
did not touch.

But today I passed
and *all* was gone,
tent, fence, occupant—
The winds were
gone and the green
was calm.

Did you, clean-up crew,
like thieves
that come at night
to steal
the ammunition of the wind,
the broken limbs
and traffic signs,
the loose comforts
of unanchored lives,

did you steal the home
of a homeless man
or woman
the wind had made its own?

The Bodies of Everest

To the two hundred bodies still
on the mountain—

Men built mountains
once
of brick and bitumen
to bring god down to us—
Only the dead
know *this* peak's
otherworldliness.

Only they know
the winter dark
on these slopes of ice and snow,
hear airless winds
cry *holy holy holy*
and feel its granite shake.

Their lounged or sprawling bodies
watch you pass
the high crevasses
as if from settees
in the cold's embrace.
This mountain's made
them its own.

We push ourselves
because we can;

we're drawn to life's
questions
because they're there,

but these faceless forms,
honed by peaks
and their zastrugal
sleep,
speak with the larynx of silence:

You who leave
climbed only a mountain,
we who stayed
surmounted ourselves . . .

Pawnee Grasslands

Six a.m., California Zephyr

When dawn rays
lie flat on
Pawnee grasslands,
and no shadows exist,

this is the best time
to be awake,
the best place
to be awake—

How two things
separate,
how like the sun
one rises,

how like the earth
one stops,
how wakeful
they contend,

and how alternate they cease.
Now faith
and life-world find
agreeable rest.

Grail Train

I bought the tickets
so far in advance,
I forgot the destination,
but by the time
the station was reached,
I was certain *this* train
would take us somewhere.

I have been surrounded
by pornography so long—
so much passionless loving
become such passionate
self-pleasuring—
that I needed a vacation.

Garbage of homeless camps
slide by the window.
Rape and a fist are the only
honest relationships.
The people who love
children the most
are not their parents.
When the fountain is dry,
it's soon covered in graffiti.

Lovers play hook-up roulette,
dismiss those who love them,
cling to those who don't—

And always in their ears
the grinding of bearings
with one insidious question:
is she the best you can do?
People who thirst
drink from glasses of sand.

Limp men throng gun-ranges,
fraudulent women
shoot flash-bulb smiles.
All over the country
husbands and wives
embrace with the conviction
of dancing instructors.
Women send us on missions.
At night everything itches.

The female body is perilous.
A neon sign twitches
over shadows
where silhouettes stalk
and cars slow
and sometimes stop.
This chapel
wasn't made for weddings.

Sparrow of the Sea

Somewhere between Antigua and St Maarten

Those sea-birds plunge
stuka-wing, or
hang on pillars in the air,
but the sparrow in the solarium
will die out of doors,
this far from land.

Little sparrow, hopping
among plastic leaves,
do you still pine
for that tepid breeze
that blew you so far
from home?

You will be cold
if you leave
when we anchor again,
far to the north
where it's snowing today.
I will toss crumbs
on the table beside me,

and you can stay here
in your sea-roving cage,
more far-travelled
than any free bird,
and make lonely men happy
as a sparrow of the sea.

Epiphany on a Winter Day

January 30th 2019

Walking in from the parking-lot,
arctic cold carving
my cheeks into blocks of ice,
I know why the Romans
named this month
for a god of two faces:

the wind that hits me
in my forward-face,
hits me again
when I turn around,
in my backward-facing face—

So as if in mourning
for a dead world,
I bow my head
and squint through tearful eyes
at the fossilized ground . . .

Then escape within
to a sheltered hall
of perpetual greenery,
smelling of Pine Sol and
old carpets,
dead of significance.

These are not
the epiphanies of writers,
who capture a blink
of the crowd-flash
in poems of the actual,

but here or in some restroom stall,
as if out of the corner
of an unguarded eye,
in a mind turned off,
a hidden thought
jumps out from behind
a door
as you turn to close it,

an idea so new,
yet that was there all along,
surprises you—

and you suddenly know
it had noting to do
with wind,
or a time of the year . . .

Personal Christian

"And the Lord said to me, set up a placard
in the market place, and write on it in the vernacular . . . "
Isaiah 8:1

It's always a day
like today
that appears in the dream:
the last leaf
strips from the tree,

bus-stops offer
no shelter from the wind,
people feel
hemmed in by the cold,

—And I'm suddenly
homeless, and
don't know what to do.

And when I'm awake
the same streets
call out to me:
stop ignoring us—
We've tied every way
to reach you.

We appear in your dreams,
and during the day,
the same silence

seizes you
that seizes the tongues
of all who belong to us.

So it's more than the wind
that hurries me past
huddling forms
that can't talk to anyone,
but not because they can't speak.

At least they can still write.
I read their signs
with relief.
God is a Homeless Man
one says,
and I almost slow down . . .

Scenery for a Puppet-Screen

Returning from a walk, Washington, D.C.

It is dark—but I don't need to see;
I walk here often
and my legs
know the sidewalk
well enough—

So I know before I get there
what the streetlight
in the trees will show
in soft relief:

a rose still blooming
by the walk, a dark crown
and scrim of thorns,
scenery for a puppet-screen . . .

I pass grateful for the cloaking
dark, unable to behold
its wasting beauty folded
into fading colors,
like the lids of sleepy children—

I have seen summer's tide
draining, leaving pools
of color in the trees,
and pools on sidewalks under trees,
and my eyes were like sieves,
struggling to hold—

I have seen winter mornings,
headlights braiding
gold on gray uniforms,
and jewels concealing
colors in the wicker trees,
and felt the sight
receding from my eyes—

Bring me a mirror
to look at these things.
Bring me a painting.
No child drew
away his hand from the prick
of a painting—
As these are to the world,
so I am.

Ideas of Rapture for a Country Not Known to the Bible

St Charles, Missouri 1970

The problem was you could never be certain
the signs were not from the darker forces . . .
Meghan O'Gieblyn, "Interior States"

ONLY snow lights this river.
No light leaks from above,
for the moon is down,
but it is enough—the snow,
the swamp-willow,
white sycamore
and swift-flowing ice are enough . . .

Yet even this glow
does not reach
beyond the far shore . . .
a hair of trees
and indistinct hills,
too dark to be ghostly.

When it was spring
and air-tufts were blowing,
the bare boughs hazed
and driftwood piled
like cast-off crutches,

brown arms paddled
an endless canoe,

war-party returning
with booty of bedsteads
and float-away boats,
till the boiling flood
reached dreaming windows,
dreams were disturbed
and dreamers awoke
as if from a fever . . .

It no longer mattered
what physical shores
this river touched,
or where any dream
came from—
I had enough of both
to hear its song.

I DREAMED a crowd.
They stood at a pair
of bronze doors unaware
it was raining, and the
doors shone like gold.

The doors rose over their heads,
ten panels of mythical scenes,
powerfully wrought,
and the rain pouring down

on their restless umbrellas,
drilling the cobble-stones;
still they stared in awe,
thinking this was all:

the doors were ajar,
and now and then a child
slipped through . . .

IT BEGINS with a child—
and a splintered mirror,
and who will fix
the pieces of a broken face?

It begins with a fish-pond's
lily-pads and dead frogs,
a dead soup no life moves
below a lid of ice
preserving its last stare,
and a sudden star of cracks—
a sudden plunge into
numbing danger,
cold dragging of clothes.

It begins on a day
no child remembers
but every child knows,

the day of the opening
of the eyes,
small eyes become large.

WHO WILL GUIDE my thoughts
on the way of understanding?
Should I get on a bus
that sits waiting for a member
who always comes late?
Should I take a tour
to see the sights of the city?

Will I submerge in a crowd
in a great hall of beautiful walls,
and follow a fanciful
parasol floating ahead,
and cluster and strain
and not hear anything at all?

Or will I be one of the crowd
who seeks the gift-shop
and restroom and sits feet up
and looks at his watch,
and thinks only of getting ahead
and knows he won't
get anywhere here?

Something will speak to me.
Whether in the produce aisle
or in a shadow of leaves
on a wall or a dove-burst
spreading on an evening sky . . .
—Or the image of a young man
in garments of steel,
and a horse that looks down—

You almost feel
the thoughts of the youth,
and the horse beside him,
as though it too
could have thoughts,

filled for a moment
with the treble of a bird,
(for he has made room
for all but himself),
or a ripple among leaves,
or just the forest's total
timeless yes to life,

where the coming-in and
going-out of being,
like a shuffling deck,
blur in a moment
that stands still forever,

(for he has made himself
like that which he seeks).
Then with the gentlest shake,
closes himself and goes on . . . .

I SEE REASON for hope
in the ill-manner of Americans.
Their racism delights me.
I approve the hate
that is placed with the salt-shaker.
We brought our hate
with us in the holds
of our ships,
and found fertile soil
for strains of our own.

I think of a story—
It is the first story of stories.
It is the story of how
a couple were kicked
out of somewhere delightful,
and straight-away their children
began killing each other.

But it is no story—
We are their descendents
and that is our history.

For are we not worse
than a red-headed step-child,

full of envy and blame,
for whom no law
is too strict to control—?
And some would call us
existential and others
bastards of creation,

whether rejected at birth,
—or rejected in person,
who refused to conform
their person—

or merely the well-born
heirs of good parents
too delicate to recall
all humankind's heroes
were unwanted children,
or raised by wolves . . .

Some grew up stuttering,
who didn't have
confidence to speak,
didn't stand up for themselves
because they didn't
have authority to stand,

grew up to be craven
pleasers of bad people,
who didn't have permission
to be who they were,
and gave themselves permission,
and still felt like frauds—

I watch a waitress
light a cigarette
in the last booth in the back
and blow smoke
to the side like dry snow,
and I in my own booth
draw on a cigarette
of my thoughts . . .

How we accepted nothing because
nothing accepted us,
questioned everything
because we are entirely questionable,
believed in no god but
joined any cult that would have us,
and grew disillusioned
and dropped out
and joined again anyway,

and realized too late
we were only invalidating ourselves,
completing in ourselves

what nature had started,
and maybe we *were*
of the world after all,
no bastards of anything—
And looked out a window
and felt doubly fraudulent . . .

NOT EVERYTHING is a door
but when you've had to
go through enough of them,
everything starts
to look like a door,
and I guess nothing's lost
by treating them as doors,
every friend a door
to a new self, every day
a door to a new life—

And many words have been
written over doors,
and few have been good,
and two doors have no words
anyone can read,
and the last thing anyone wants
is to go through a door
not of their choosing . . .

But one door has these words:
Beyond this door all answers are.
It is at this door I pause—

This is the door that is
around every corner.
This is the door through
which everyone goes.
The more despairing they are,
the more often they go.

People pray on their problems
and having been trained
to pay attention and
not let their guard down
like the disciples who slept,
see billboards as doors
and messages in cookies
and answers in crows
under thunder clouds
and on license plates,

because fools could speak
wisdom and beggars
angels in disguise,
and the God who is with us
is playing a game for garden-gnomes . . .

But there is danger in signs.
Believers have to be careful.
Even the secular world
has a name for this danger.
Every door reminds us
we are plunged into lies,
and truth wanders home
with a ringing in its ears.

I AM A JOINT where body
and soul hinge—
and I hold in my hand
the knotted hip of a child
that was dislocated at birth
millennia ago,
noting the growth of the bone
as it twisted and fused
and tried to heal itself—
till the girl died and brought
healing to an end,
or finally succeeded
if you prefer it that way . . .

And I don't care what you call it,
it wasn't anybody's fault.
I believe the girl grew
to love running and jumping,

and didn't blame herself
because she couldn't run too—

No children are where I work
and that's a blessing—
Buses pull up and let down
their elevator-doors
and their freights unload,
of whom I cannot speak
without violating some
standard of decency
more basic than privacy,

but I will tell you they
come wearing helmets
and some in recliners
with towels around their necks
and a woman whose legs
are like baobab trunks
that root with each step,
and others for whom life
was a color and
they don't have any left . . .

After a quick rain the sun
sharpens its conclusions
with a brilliance that leaves
no shade for my thoughts:

that they brought it on themselves,
didn't exercise enough,
didn't quite smoking,
ate nothing but junk food—

But even without clarity
nothing is dark enough
to hide what you do,
thinking you're not like them,
it can't happen to you—

Someday all sicknesses
will finally be cured, but there is
no cure for *this* sickness.

We don't own who we are.
We have no claim to press,
can't back ourselves up—
We might as easily be them,
and maybe we will be
in the next life, and
maybe this is what it means,
being driven out naked . . .
being driven out naked . . .

NOW IS the time—
the time between deaths,
a time to cross and re-cross
a street, to find the side
that strangely fits,
a time to know the tar-pit
of the self, hiding in every
shadow of a sunny day,
a time to know the plunge
of shame beside
the punch-bowel, while
people still make punch,
a time for end-time beliefs
and calming stones,
a time for meditations—

Did the fathers of this country
dream in their homes
of finding something old?
Did they think to search
new lands for what eluded
them at home, already
a thousand years outworn,
known from a story in gold?

Or did they bring it anyway
like rats
gnawing their hawsers,

(*and some did—and ended*
afraid of each other, and
put up bodies like scarecrows
to swing in the wind,)
that with that tale they too
could outlast the world,
change a living form
for the image of a form,
like fresh paint trapped
in a chapel's plaster,
and dying go unbended
into stiff earth,
and cold into colder graves . . . ?

But I hear a different sound
from your withering coal-towns,
I hear a sound
from your emptying main-streets:
the body leaves you
like a disappointed friend,
or just forgets your name
before it goes,
returning to its world
like a drop to a downpour . . .

Leaves fall like playing-cards
and appear again like cards,
and the seasons

shuffle them together,
and like face-cards
people wander through
on hiking-trails,
and over a bridge where
couples stand,
the shuffling forest holds a tent;
a slight rain dimples
the air,
and fleshless shadows circulate
beneath their feet . . . .

I HAVE TRIED to explain
these things;
nothing have I understood.

You have made yourself
what you seek,
whether a personal truth
or a philosopher's truth,
a Christian truth
or a Buddhist truth—

And I have stood
in a summer storm,
and watched leaves torn

and umbrellas like
blossoms borne down
sudden streams,
and some running
and others
Spartan in the uninvited rain,

and given thanks
in a doorway
for a dry place to stand,
and looked out
at a generous world,

and saw the sky
unfold its own flag,
its fan of all colors—
after rain in the desert . . .

David Churchill

Homeless on Sidewalk

The sidewalk is hard,
but it makes life soft,
when I lay my cheek
on its grime,
and close my eyes
to the rainfall of feet,

because it's rent-free,
and I live nowhere
of rent—
Not to be blameless
do I wander the streets

like a sparrow,
trash-cans my gutter,
talking to invisible
flocks—
I am provisioned
for the street
like the starling and grackle,

but make no mistake.
I feed puffed
or flapping
pigeons from my hand,
through no fault
of my own . . .

Carnival Pier

Ocean City Amusement Pier, Maryland 2018

Watch the seagull fly
from far off skies,
to build its nest
in the Ferris-wheel.
Donovan

Let's go to the carnival pier,
an electric jewel-box
spilled in the sea—
It has something to offer
at every age.

Children love it,
they get to stay up
after dark;
adolescents get permission
to go without parents;
couples hold each other tight;
the lonely take a break
from the weight
of themselves

for one more night.
And here and there
a few gray forms
too old to be children again
turn mottled faces
toward the lights,

feel its sparkle on their skin
like cooling fronds,
wonder where the time went,
and was it worth it,
after all:

after the cries and the tumult,
after the crowds,
after the tilt-a-wheel—
to see an empty seat
go around,
and drifting in the glow
a piece of down.

On First Looking into Ken Burns' Civil War

October, 2018

Imagine a palette
of dusky colors
that still manage to glow,
set in a luminous sky,

for these are days
that are made in heaven,
and we have had
a heavenly autumn,

—yet on looking back,
it seems now every day
was dressed in black . . .

for I have also been looking
into a civil war,
and black is a good color
for pictures of clothes
with bodies in them,

where men have torn
their buttons off,
looking to see
where they were shot
before they died,

and impure white
to make the black stand out—

And many are the pictures
of Andersonville,

but thank God none
of a place called Pillow,
where the men themselves
were black, and
what was done
was more than black.

Thus I here conclude
and sternly warn:
take care what day
you first begin,
for I too am hatefully black,

and I pray to see
what they forgot
when they buried the dead:
all the hate
put under ground,
before it spread.

On Hearing the Bells of the Shrine of the Immaculate Conception while Crossing a Parking-Lot

They ring at noon,
the bells in the spire
of the Shrine,
across a highway and
an intersection
and several miles of cars,

letting us know
the engineers of existence
are still at their posts,
guarding the coast
of the unknown.

In an earlier age
they called us to offer
liturgical thoughts,
but today,
as I unlock the car,
I note more
a whining complaint
rising over the roads

than the toning of bells,
from where I heard
once

the vowels of a pope
tossed over the treetops . . .

—Unless it be to think
how like a bell
a life-time is,
making its transit
from stroke to stroke,

and what that transit
might be—
a ferry from shore to shore,
an argument
from point to point,
or sometimes only
like a clock,
from hour to hour,

until that final ring-note,
whether for cook
or sequin stringer,
lost on a quivering sky . . .
finds its way home.

Thanksgiving, 2017

Olmi Landreth Drive, Alexandria, Virginia

I give thanks in my own way,
standing outside at the car—
thanks for the dark and quiet,
for the slow sweep
of the one street-light
that dresses the scene,
and for the excuse to step out

to get away from inside,
from an atmosphere
too thick to breathe,
and the company steep
as the path on a Peruvian hill—

There's a name for this condition,
but I know what I am
so I don't use it for myself:
I am a man who makes excuses
to step out from a crowd,

to take a gasp of cold air
to carry back to the body
inside, to last till I leave—
back to the family at the table,

buoyed on their likenesses
as though wine were a lake—

where smiles are too wide
and greetings too loud
and lips creak struggling
to stretch and scrape,
and something is wrong
with the popcorn—

and I don't care what you call it.
—As long as someone
remembers the errand
I announced,
till I turn to go back,
undisturbed by search-parties . . .

But as the night breathed in
and settled a wing,
a man appeared,
walking down the road,
and disappeared—like a
reflection in a darkened room

where hidden mirrors pass
an image from an unknown source:
broken shoes, no socks,
no underclothes beneath
a double-breasted suit,
hurrying as if condemned
to walk an unknown

number of streets,
and wanting to get it done—

And as the night
re-absorbed this vision,
longer than I care to admit,
my retinas refused
to let him go . . . .

Is there something
that issues a call—?
I suppose it has a name.
They are like hermits in reverse,
set out of sight
in the midst of us,
as if in a bubble
in a circus crowd—
Their truth is the street.
When they go there, they appear.

When I was sure
I had thought
him out of existence again,
I turned and went in.

The Stages of Awake

It is time to wake up but
your mind wants to sleep—
That's how it begins.

They say Nietzsche invented
the Eternal Return of the Same,
life after life
for the rest of eternity;
as you try to get up
you know what he meant.

So you turn off
the mechanical rooster—
and try not to think
of the Four Last Things:
a man rubbing his eyes,
unaware bull-dozers
are coming to pave
over his grave
for that parking-lot in paradise.

Before the mirror
in the bathroom,
the first words of the morning arrive:
Noli me tangere,
I have not yet risen—

Grownup eyes were the first mirror,
where your prattle froze
in grownup frowns.
For the first time
you saw what
being snail-eyed looked like—
And became an adult,
hardly out of diapers;

and later, with eyes un-averted,
you looked at someone
you loved
and saw what *they* were,
and felt a new kind of shame.

All night you were turning
the pages of a book
in a language
you didn't understand—
Now in the light
of day you see:
there is no mystery
in headlines of the world.

Who are you now
after so many stages?
You are a traveler
with too many passports.

Let others worry
about who they are now.
You float through security
without ringing a bell.

Conversations with Stones

Walters Art Museum, Classical Collection, Oct 1, 2017

These are not
the calcified concaves of bodies
filled in with plaster,
but remains of people
nonetheless—

Even these gods once
were people:
tidy slave girl holding
a too-heavy spear,
helmet crushing
sun-bleached tresses,
while some chalky sculptor
molds Athena—

That torso of Apollo,
the latest darling of the games,
still reaching to rub
dust on his palms,
still a little out of breath—

A sailor from Piraean docks,
whose deep-set eyes
still scan
for distant storms,
models the head of Odysseus—

Outside the window
the sun dims—
Is *this* their underworld,
this dusty hall,
these drifting motes
dimming in bloodless beams?

Even we like shadows
keep restful silences,
glad to be so
close to so much life,
—and no closer . . .

Wherein the Writer Addresses Himself in the Next Life

"The eternal hourglass of existence is turned
upside down again and again, and you with it . . . "
Nietzsche

To myself in the year three thousand,
when I will be you—
unless you have already
been born again
before I die,
the new you drawing
the life out of me,
transparent to thready veins
and a faltering heart—

For it may be
you are already born
before I die,
like a butterfly emerging
from its mold,
neither wholly in
new body or out—

But whether you wait
or so eager to begin,
would rob an old man
of his last breath,
don't think you
make a fresh start;
nothing starts from zero.

It will be on a day
when trees sway to each other,
a page will
blow across your path,
and you will know
when you pick it up
and think
I can do better than this—

For it is not for you
to do what I did,
but to carry the work on:
for that is my wish
as I tear out this page
and discard it to the wind.

What else will you need to know:
my private ground
already covered,
challenges left unmet,
tests of character deferred,
struggles carried over
for another round, or lost—?

Some see statehouse domes
reflecting in Bauhaus glass,
gothic spires
shading subway stairs—

You will see *your* past
in the faces around you,
in the eyes of those
who already seem to know you.

David Churchill

Stopping in the Night to Let a Freight Pass

The Capital Limited, Washington to Chicago

The gliding stops.
The same slope
that slid you down
to sleep
now slides you back.

The idea jolts you.
No—it is the night
that gives a jump—
Now you are stopped.

Silence.
Creak of arthritic trucks,
cabin air shush.
No toads croak
in this embalming dark.

Is this what being
alone is?
If the sun rose now,
you still wouldn't know
where you were,
still wouldn't move.

And the sun *doesn't* rise—
The darkness extends.

Moment by moment
confidence ebbs . . .

What's taking so long?
When will we
move again?
Why don't we move?

We must move, always.
Blood must move,
thoughts move,
time move . . .

—Or am I dead
and this death,
all rush and no motion?

Death is a Crowd

If you took all the dead
whose faces appear
in the obituaries,
you would have enough faces
to fill a ballroom.

How do friends
find each other there?
Or is everyone
friends now—
the cheater and the
faithful wife,
the bully and the cripple,
the baby and
the bruising boyfriend,
all redeemed . . . ?

Christians will tell you
we'll be unaware
of each other,
all looking at God—
But why do we
love one another now,
if not practicing for something?

And what of the introvert,
the crowd-shy,
the one who

crosses the street
to avoid someone he knows—?

Will he still be able
to hide in his skin?

David Churchill

On a Refusal to Convict a Low-Level Drug Dealer While the Sacklers Endow Another Museum

Jury Duty, Washington, DC 2018

He sits directly across from me,
Daquan—or something—
A bearded young man; give him
a boater and white skin

and he could be Amish.
The judge reads the charges.
I hear but don't hear.
I hear the rustle of a Grecian

breeze through silver trees,
watch shadows slant across stone.
We sit in the area
reserved for the chorus.

I'm sure a breeze sighs
through coal-town hollows too,
when coal-trains racket by,
where barbecue grills and old cars

rust from the inside out,
and American-flag curtains
grow stiff in trailer-park windows . . .
The cause of all sighs

sifts down from on high.
There the petals of a thornless rose
perfumes white halls,
where the bodies of gods
gather like clouds
on a day that does not rain.

In vain let the young man
come forth for destruction—
In vain do we cry:
how can there be justice,
without a capital J?

David Churchill

Turkey Vulture Warming Wings in Mendocino County, California

Family Reunion, 2018

Mornings come with too-early
precision—
already a Charybdis
of voices in the kitchen.

Family is a vortex
in this house,
rising like the sun
toward day, leaving
ten-mile day-hikes
in dark canyons below.

What do they think
in those bottom-lands?
Do hikers grow short
under redwoods,
shame to turn
dwarvish faces toward light?

I slink aside,
molted of wakefulness
and still uncarapaced;
I cling to quiet corners
and distance like a rock.

But on a cypress bough outside,
an omen-bird
outspreads heraldic wings
in a summoning ray,

and my heart warms
to see its slunk head
slowly planning a day
that will not begin without him.

Western Shore

Mendocino County, CA.

When the sun goes down,
here on the coast,
the land peels its lips
and takes the sea in its teeth.

—But this sea resists.
Inchoate battles
of creation resume,
as white arms of gods
contend with unruly rocks.

Impromptu fountains fly
and geysers leap
to get out of the way.
Waves break en echelon,
but all you hear
is a continuous roar.

People leave feeling
unsettled—and a little
confused,
as though a glass wall stood
at land's end—

And drive away wishing
the view had a souvenir

stand,
they could take something home . . .

But when days fade,
people walk out on headlands,
see waves raise
church window-panes
in the setting rays,
and leave happy again.

David Churchill

Rookery, Caspar Headland

Mendocino County, California

The tide is high,
hurling white thrones
to the wind
over wine-dark rocks—
The water is a little
warmer than ice,
and the sea lions are loving it.

This is their house,
this western ledge—
Here their whiskers raise
to bark in chorus
with the wild wave spray
and the wind crush.

We are lions of the sea,
kin to the petrel
and the topsy-turvy gulls—
Here we live
and here we breed,
and feed on the salmon,
cold and free.

Forward-Looking Mind

I am old—
Time has wrapped
its tap-roots
around my hands,
poured like floods
across the gullies
of my eyes . . .

Even the memories
of the inner me
that has not changed
are losing their names.

I remember couples
in grocery stores
as if with single hands
reaching for the shelves,
living in tomorrow,
with tomorrow's meals,
tomorrow's baby care—
unless tomorrows fail,
and couples end.

But my children are grown;
my children's children,
in their childhood time,
don't yet know—

they have tomorrow
in their bones.

One will be a judge;
he will condemn
the dead-ends of behavior;
and one will be a builder;
he will build
no house to last a day—

But all will come to where I am,
to watch a larkspur bloom
and drop a leaf,
to watch a moth appear,

to watch the circle close
the sun burns through
an eyeglass frame,
to be told
to close doors
you keep leaving open behind you . . .

Angel of the Streets

They had been stealing from her
all along.
Small things at first:
a piece of cardboard,
a shoelace pair,
a mismatched pair
of hub-caps—
They thought she didn't notice . . .

You would see her at sunrise
in the Lucite
of glass-walled canyons,
then miles away
on a story-book street,
as if she really did have wings,

till finally,
under a horseman's gaze,
where streams converged
in an asphalt pool,
on a spit of sidewalk
big enough to park her carts,
she felt safe.

—Until that morning.
It was in a low hall,
cafeteria clash
crashing over huddled forms,

the smell of tomato soup
and fry grease
in the graying air—
Panic griped her heart.

I saw her again today,
caught in the cold
between corners of safety—
a holy flame
igniting her cheeks.

Her children had come back to her,
I was happy to see;
what would she be
without children—?
Balking at curbs,
lagging at crosswalks,

and how patient she turns,
rounding them up
like unmindful ducklings . . .

Visit to the Museum of the Bible

Washington DC, February 27th, 2018

I carried my journal
to the Museum of the Bible,
and came out again blank
as its pages, still
blank—

Not writing down
the brass doors
ten stories tall
like the tablets of the law
through which I passed,

nor the floor of Heaven
over the downward
eyes of the crowd,
and its hundred and fifty seven
kaleidoscopes of glory—

Only aware of a healing cold
and long shadows
wrapping the streets
up for the night
when I came out.

My brain like a bell that keeps ringing
was empty,
a space where

noise of the crowd
resounded:

choirs of faces,
crush of wheelchairs
and crutches,
and other things
too much to take in—

And my journal,
with its pages like prayers,
flapping like a bird
with no gifts for the sky.

Some only wanted
their faith to be whole,
others wanted
their bodies restored—
As for me,
the whole world
is a place of blindness
and confusion.

Where is a museum
for the quiet
that amplifies silence?
Let us go there
to be together,

and write our prayers
down on paper.

Name of the Name

Do you have a name
for God?
Some call him No-End,
others, I-Am-That-I-Am,
still others, Most-High.

I call him Answer.
He is the answer
to the question we ask:
Why is there something
instead of nothing?

What are the powers of Answer?
Nobody knows.
Nobody knows
if he has any powers.
All we can know
are the powers that are our own.

One thing we know:
Answer must be
a God who creates life.
If this weren't true,
how could there be
any questions at all?

But are we not only
like a glint of the sun,

that though the waves
be numerate
and time be infinite,
the light that glints
on the wave now,
will never glint again—?

Better some questions
never be answered,
than some questions exist
that don't find their answer
in Answer.

David Churchill

The Ten Thousand Pass the Ruins of Nineveh

And it shall come to pass, that all they that look
upon thee shall flee from thee, and say, Nineveh
is laid waste: who will bemoan her? whence shall I
seek comforters for thee?
Nahum, 3:7

The thunder happened first,
then the strike—
Five men cut down, unarmed,
under a flag of truce
while we slept.
The news shattered our camp.

No watch set, men
scattered where they dropped,
fires cold,
the horses unfed,
a cry of mourning spreading
wide across the plain
for leaders lost,
a trust betrayed,
our homeland receding
before our eyes—

That night when sleep
like a fickle lover came,
in a dream I saw
my father's house,
its door-posts fallen,

stables empty,
goat-herd squatters in the court-yard—
Then the night lit up
and eardrums burst,
the house left flaming.

Now three days and nights
we pass these hills
of crumbling stone,
heading north—
hear the keening wind
annoyed at chinks,
the chatter of jackdaws,
whispers of a restless dust,
among shadows
of a city's derelict gods . . .

What was this place
that takes three days to pass?
What walls of
interlocking stones,
what garrison of weeds?
What voice of prophets singing,
as if from tombs?

I am the ruins of Nineveh,
den of the lion and throne of a god—
Why have I been deserted?

Did I not sit on ashes for Jonah?
Out of such places
new worlds have risen.
Why have the soldiers forgotten me?

NOTES: "From this place they marched one stage, six parasangs, to a great stronghold, deserted and lying in ruins. The name of this city was Mespila[1], and it was once inhabited by the Medes. The foundation of its wall was made of polished stone full of shells, and was fifty feet in breadth and fifty in height."

---

1. The ruins which Xenophon saw here were those of Nineveh, the famous capital of the Assyrian Empire. It is curious to find him dismissing this great Assyrian city with the casual and misleading statement that "it was once inhabited by the Medes." In fact, the capture of Nineveh by the Medes (c. 600 B.C.) was the precise event which closed the important period of its history, and it remained under the control of the Medes only during the succeeding half-century, i.e. until the Median Empire was in its turn overthrown by the Persians (549 B.C.). Xenophon, then, goes but one unimportant step backward in his historical note—perhaps because he did not care to go farther, perhaps because he was unable to do so.

Lamentation for a Friend

Jennifer Moore Crocker 1945 - 2017

A condor on a useless ledge,
scanning low clouds
out of pinpricks
of hunger
for propitious weather,
too big to soar without wind . . .

An albatross,
lonely for hurricanes
and no sight of land,
still hoping to soar
high enough for never
coming down,
too wide-winged to walk
on still ground . . .

I walk the streets while
the world's at work,
counting boots
on cars and plucking
starling feathers
from the ground.
A light has gone out
behind these doors:
someone who lived here
is gone,
and life is deserted . . .

Somewhere below ground,
past the point where
Eurydice turned back,
in a cavern unclothed
men cast lots—
If you win a lamp
with a sphinx for a base,
throw it back,
its wiring is faulty.

I too was one of those,
happy just to feel
a small wind
in my lungs;
a blank page under my head—

Check my decay,
count the worms in my mouth,
fix with backward
precision
the moment of death:

I once lived on gemstones,
unable to eat clay . . .

Dinner Party with Saints

Rescue: Freedom International
Hay Adams Hotel, Washington DC
December 2015

They gathered in a place
of liveried opulence,
a charitable elite:
rich in smiles
and glittering hands,
as if someone had opened
a reliquary,

the glint of polished minerals
on cuff-link
and pulse-point
rich as crosiers,

and when they sat down
to dine,
the glow from plates
framed their heads
like haloes.

These were the highest
elite,
and some held hands,
and others guided
their wives
and pulled out a chair

and tucked them in—
And like shadows
of worshipful hands
dipping in an aurora
of treasure,
I seemed to see
inside their lives
as their chatter ascended,
then slowly fell . . .

Above their heads,
as if an acid vision
on a too-white screen,
with the coffee
and dessert,
the rescued women spoke.

They spoke of the rules
of love,
how much was paid
for a partner's time,
who came
and who went,
and how it was handled.

The woman beside me
made a request,

easily answered,
rewarded with a smile.

The touch of her hand on mine
was as light
as the wing of a sparrow,
clasping the sky.

Then we left.
A man wrote out
a check,
and a woman was drunk . . .

David Churchill

The Greatest Generation in the Year Two Thousand

Memorial Day, 2000

Chalk on sidewalk—
and an ideal lack of children.
A midweek summer calm
sustains the gray-green moment,
before the first
less-than-gust disturbs
the glyphs.
They lift like
butterflies into the future.
Spreading rainspots
chase them off.

The rain falls in a silence
not of its making.
Roads have drained the life
of this street.
The houses are silent.
The rain ticks softly
on handicapped parking
and blind child signs.

—Even a stooped form
and a quaking Chihuahua,
relics of another age,
with all the time now
to wait on life's needs,
sustain the nothing.

He remembers stars
being born in the void
beneath him,
search-lights announcing
the opening of a new galaxy;
you could almost hear
the hymns
of the *Volkesdeutsche*
in their basements below . . .
But all that happened
a long time ago,
and in a different country.

It is the last act of a journey,
an unlikely end,
echoed in the thunder
of a summer rain.
If you were there now
you too would give thanks
to have come out again
on this island of calm.

A normal rain
falls now on grateful trees,
and sidewalk colors
curl in full gutters.
Worms flush out in fat laces,

and people summon
courage for a walk.

A blaze of rain-gems
will tell you
the rainfall has ceased.
Look for a proscenium
arch, propped
against a cloud,
and maybe a new curtain:

one age has ended;
an age of changes
has begun.

Cruise with Humanity

Grandeur of the Sea, January, 2017

They come on board
pushing walkers and canes,
drive up the gangway
in motorized scooters,
or struggle along
on unsteady legs—
Once we're at sea,
we'll all be needing walkers.

These are a people
doubly blessed—
Their careers are built
and their children grown.
Their reward now
is a balcony suite
and a final decade
of grotesque decay.

Some live here now,
a sea-going home,
others are taking
a vacation from old.
Their hardest task now
is to fight for a place
at a never-ending buffet,
to put on a little more flesh

to slow time's
whittling away . . .

I do not ask how
many pouches
these cargo-thighs can hold,
or how loose
these pajamas of skin
have grown—
I ask if the core
of their relationships is strong.

Your daughter and son,
do they withdraw
from what you've become?
Your grandchildren
whom you love,
do you even remember
their names?
That matchbox of words
you used to share
with your wife,
is it empty at last?

Outside the windows
life's boil of lapis
lazuli is desperate
to return to a solid.

A sapphire sky
volatilizes freedom.
Tell me, Humanity—
is there energy left
to visualize a nephew?

Mothers' Day

Almost every
woman I know
is a mother,
which could be a lot,
depending on how you count:
some I remember,
some I don't,
some I forgot—

But this I didn't forget:
the walk in the rain,
carrying a box
and a pot of geraniums,

and planting the box
under the geraniums,
at the end of the walk—

It felt good to get
the earth on my hands,
then stand
and make the motion
of palms
that means *there, that's done . . .*

—Suddenly a desire
to break out of these words—
Not make sense

at all anymore—
Escape reason entirely—

Talk instead about
the flower
of the slowly blooming
cactus—
or nothing at all.

But the pitfalls
of sharing a body
and a cry
that isn't answered
constrain me . . .

Only later, walking back,
did I realize
how light that
little box had been,
how near
to the ground,
but how hard to put down—

The fear of infants
in unsafe arms
means nothing,
the danger

of boyfriends
means nothing—

The earth too
puts forth its cures
in years,
like a small flower
that blooms
from an unfeeling root,

to find another source
of love,
to no longer fear
life's birth after birth.

I hope for a cure
for final earth—
So I can choose again,
and choose you again . . .

Temple with Sphinxes

Scottish Rite Temple
16th St NW Washington DC

A long time ago
a strip-mall gypsy
cupped my palm
in her palm,
looked at the wall and said

you were born to be good,
you were born to be bad,
you were born to be sad.

Ever since then
I've been looking
for that wall,
and I think I have found it.

On a street in a city:
a flight of steps,
two sphinxes
and a door
I have never seen open.

It is useless to seek something
that can never
be known,
unless we seek it
as a friend—

So as if asking a friend,
I ask of these sphinxes,
what can we know,
what questions
can we ask,
to what do we relate
when we relate to existence?

The orbs of those
stone eyes stare back—
Only one answer
seems to come
from their sockets:
don't think you know us,
just because you talk to us.

It is not the answer
I expect from a friend.
But I know
what this friend
expects from me:

to stand and be present,
keep faith
with silence,
keep the relationship
honest.

Aquarius

"Mystic crystal revelation
And the mind's true liberation . . . "
Fifth Dimension, *The Age of Aquarius*

They called us existential people—
those double-breasted
foreign men who
broke our gust of arms that
blew along the sidewalk,
old-world stumps
our laugh bemused,
who watched us pass
that winter hour . . . .

Do you remember that night?
Store-fronts bright
under bare trees,
slow ambers and blues
on traffic poles
regulating flows of leaves
across carless streets . . . ?

They looked after us,
a new kind of youth,
wind arranging our hair
or running with a scarf,
throw-away clothes
warm enough for our bones,
then turned again
to their foreign consciousness,

to their city of monuments
crackling in the cold,
their mansions of power,
glittering like icebergs . . .

But we did not observe.
Our unawareness
like the darkness
was coated in glitter-dust,
crystal spectacles
unlocking insane faith-dreams
of innocence and freedom.

The sun had risen
as if from under our feet,
in-breaking out of
tract-house families
sitting down to rote dinners
in the shadow of tv glare,

among green lawns
and two-tone cars,
where ignorant boys
pushed pioneer logs
and girls hugged pale dolls,

and when crocuses bloomed
in new snow,

were surprised to find
ourselves still alive,
already contingent enough,
already like mayflies
taking wing for one day,
and every day was that day—

To live for being high
without being straight,
for being awake
without being asleep,
for being hungry
without being fed,
for being in love
without being in hate . . .

Do you remember the night
our brains were kaleidoscopes,
and we ran to a church—
and the doors were locked?
What kind of people
lock their churches at night?

We stared through the doors,
saw the altar inside—
In vain does a church
try to lock people out:
the revelation was inside!

David Churchill

Echo Lake

Winthrop Lake District, Maine

Come with me—
I know a lake in Maine
where we can paddle
out on still water
when the sun is down,
and stare up at stars
like a sparkle blanket,
so thick you suffocate—

There's no one there
but loons that sing
their lonely song,
and water plash
of soundless oar,
no light along the shore;
two souls adrift,
a little afraid of stars
they've never seen
burning so bright before.

Before we leave,
look up one last time—
Let me see in your eyes
what science knows,
how this star-flash
burns its imprint
on our nerves,

and our souls are
snow-globes,
swirling with a galaxy
of everything that is,

for even we are only
neurons sparkling
in each other's minds—
But if neurons
can ask a question,
let me ask you mine:
if lovers wander
endless halls,
what are the stars themselves,
that wind dimensions
around the spindles of
their flame,
an imprint of?

David Churchill

Petals in the Cold

Spring came in February
this year—magnolia
blossoms on campus trees'
bare boughs, dogwood
blossoms in white clouds,

then the soft grass suddenly
froze, and squirrels made
sharp stirrings again
on winter walkways,
and the wind hardened again
out of arctic halls.

I did not linger long,
staring at this new palette
of pinks and grays, but
hurried on, too cold
to conclude much
about life and death,
except to note a season
out of season—

But all day long
I had the strangest feeling,
and days after that,
stopping at every window,
asking myself
what am I looking at . . . ?

What's so strange
about the soft and greeny
flush of blossoms,
set off in stainless cold?
—Unless it be that
nature let its costume slip,
showed itself
the stereopticon it is?

Inauguration Day

January 20th, 2017

It would be known
as a compromise day:
wet streets, a sky
the color of bruised eyes,
holiday trees still
scenting the curbs with
discarded balsam—
While on one block bright
as day,
on another, night black,
combining in grey . . .

It was a day that went everywhere
at once,
like a compass
without a needle.
Yet everyone agreed,
all felt a pull
in one direction or another—

A band from coal-town
told me
God was their compass,
elbows turning
like weather vanes,
spats a-splash
and shakos nodding,
in step with the Lord . . .

Yet on other streets
a beast was unleashed,
and people struggled
to contain it
in violence and darkness
and the smoke
of burning cars,
and no one spoke
the name of the beast,
for the name
was a hard name—

For others it would be known
as a day to stay in.
Those who had
cats understood
as they picked up pieces
of a puzzle it took
a year to complete,

and those who had children
watched a city of
Legos demolished,
and felt sad anyway—
and someone
with a chess-board
acknowledged
no evil was in the pawns . . .

So it continued to be
a day that pleased no one.
Pigeons scattered
without a sense of direction.

The Good is a magnet
that knows only
one thing—

We are a shock of rain
on empty bleachers,
the logic of small crowds . . .

Women's March

January 21th, 2017, the day after.

It began with a tremor
underground,
where trains were lining up,
unaware it was night,
and spread soon
to the streets,
where silent buses
pulled around corners
into the sleeping Capital,
and was answered
by a rumble in the sky
where mechanical eagles
were gathering
as if to a roost.

The sun rose on
cloud-canvas
and a monument was its pole,
and a crusade formed
and a tsunami flowed
and its signs
were like a village,
and a cry rose
like an angel in the desert,
till the city ran out of streets,
and still they kept coming,
and they took care of each other.

Night came and America
was changed.
People went home
with a question
in their hearts:

America, what are you?
Are you an idea?
Are you a state of mind?
Are you a spirit
or a way
like the way of the Tao?
America, are you Zen?

Where are your Shriner parades
and no black faces,
and drive-ins
and wigwam motels
and names ending in "luxe"
and candy-colored
ray-gun style
cars cruising endless
California freeways?

Among the silent barricades
and piles of signs,
the memory
of a woman's eyes,

with irises like turbine blades,
promised to explain.

Sea Day

Somewhere in the South Atlantic

If these ridges and troughs
had been a continent,
our pioneers
would have gone mad,
pushing westward
over changing land.

Even today
in the houses of our country,
you see the swings
on the porches
where their descendents grow drowsy,
remembering terrain.

But these are not hills
and we are not on land.
We are watching errant sprays
leaping up joyous,
and waves
clapping white hands.

For a moment
we could be on a *krater*
in a glass case,
an eye on the bow
and waves playing
like dolphins,

making you feel safe
if you fell overboard.

The same swells still
throw up their backs
like the steeds of Poseidon,
bucking at the reins.

No wonder sailors
return to the sea,
watch water turn ethereal,
live like saints
in the auras of prisms.

David Churchill

After Handel's *Messiah* Sing-Along

December 27th, 2016

Maybe it was the sky that morning,
pried open by the sun,
showing its rosy
nacre like a shell,
as if a light had never
opened before . . .

Or maybe the air,
so clear its objects
were jewels
set off in their distances,
so you too,
somehow,
felt set off in yourself . . .

Or maybe the bushes,
sociable with squirrels,
and acorns like crumbs,
made you realize
how crumbs
were an echo of summer . . .

Or maybe because
walking to work
from the lot was
something you did
every day

in your sleep,
and you weren't asleep now . . .

Exactly the moment
to feel your soul
slip its rail—

And did you wonder,
later,
when you unlocked
your office
and poured your coffee
and signed on
your computer,
and felt like yourself again,
last night's choral
replaying in your mind,

how for a moment
you had felt
like a vibration on the air?

How like tines
in a music box,
something so solid
had once been a song . . . ?

David Churchill

Street Scene Pastoral

Harvard St & Georgia Ave, NW
December 5th 2016

A tangle of dry leaves
blew into the intersection—
and turned into sparrows,
wings struggling, beaks
fencing—

Mating, in December . . . ?
No, when the birds
righted, only one was on top,
and it was no sparrow.

And the sparrow
lay still in the other
bird's clutch,
and was borne out of battle
and danger of cars,
as if by a valkyrie,

to the side of the street
where I sat behind the wheel,
not something you see
every day in a city,
trying to stay alive
by paying its bills . . .

The light changed—
but before I drove on,
I saw God-In-The-World
in the eyes of the sparrow,
and the little bird
of prey,
whatever it was . . .

Moon So Bright

Supermoon, November 14th, 2016

Tonight the moon is big,
close and bright,
its Buddha-face,
whose Buddha-belly
gives good luck when rubbed,

a calming presence
on our leaves and
evergreens
this night of darkness,
a parent bending
for a good-night kiss.

Benevolent moon,
bending to human affairs,
would any faith
be possible
had you worn instead
a jackal face,

or an ivory skull
or snake observing
every move,
or a lady saint,
weeping over sins?

Dogs stumble on
family steps,
returning from patrols,
and weary forms
turn faces home,
or to silent pairs
in happy-hour bars,
where the hour
is neither happy,
nor only an hour . . .

The sun is far tonight.
Still I could endure
another life,
to see this other
face of kindness
show itself above our streets . . .

Homeless in Wheelchair

Homeless in wheelchair,
almost too much
to bear—
Unable to walk
is already
to be homeless,
unhoused from ambulation . . . .

Add to that
no place to go.
But at least he can sit
while he goes,
knee-walking
across an intersection
while cars wait . . .

While other grim men
and women
push their life-holds
in grocery carts,
he is his own
salvage as he
turns around now
and kicks himself backward . . .

A chair on wheels,
good furniture
for one who loves

freedom;
if he gets any more free,
he'll have to walk on his hands.

Road Trip

to Jenni, who disappeared on the Internet . . .

Und als plötzlich jäh
der Gott sie anhielt und mit Schmerz im Ausruf
die Worte sprach: Er hat sich umgewendet -,
begriff sie nichts und sagte leise: Wer?
Rainer Maria Rilke, "Orpheus. Eurydike. Hermes"

The miles are solving
their invisible sums
on the odometer,
the window is open and the wind
is riding shotgun,
the sky is blue and the road is unrolling.
If the road is not unrolling,
we are not in America.

America, your linoleum
and polished concrete
that are everywhere the same
have made you invisible—
Your ceiling tiles
are too industrial to be seen,
your dairy-cases
and florescent skies
and drive-through faces
and miles of roadside
have abolished my gaze—
I have gone blind

in a room without walls.
America, sometimes I can't even
find myself anymore—

Everywhere, people are asking:
America, where are you?
People who don't
know what to ask for,
are asking.
The blood in their bodies is asking,
the slack in their muscles
and an ache in their legs
is asking.
There is a silence in men's hearts only
the wind can fill
that blows over aspens.

So we got in the car
and the odometer stirred
and we saw a sign
that said this way to America.
When we arrived
I began to feel lucky.
Surely we will find
America in this place.

A deck of signs riffled our faces,
arches, clam-shells, arrows, bells,

destinations and numbers
spewed out of a sleeve
with a blast of air-brakes—
and a sign that said Breezewood
in a cloud of re-treads.

Line at men's room door,
unshaved tee-shirt men,
ball-caps on backward
and piratical bandannas—
vinyl diners and pancake houses
and busty hostess-wenches
with the wind at their backs,
serving diner-fare on steaming plates—

But America, you were not there.
There was nothing there
but an asphalt plain
and a glitter of chrome
as far as the horizon—
America, your flags
as big as football fields
and your side-swoosh cars
and tail-fin trim are gone—
America, have you always been gone?

Your five hundred miles
has become a needle

and your spoonful cooks
smack and your back-door
man wears his pants
on the ground and your two
trains running is a queer
lesbian multi-lingual country
some people don't even want to know.

So we drove again,
past a nondescript landscape
that was further than distance,
through a land
we could no longer understand,
as though it had more
dimensions than we did.
And we thought maybe
you have to give it something,
something we had lost . . .

The woman beside me was silent,
wrapped in the wind,
lost in her thoughts
that were plugged in like ear-buds.
She was thinking of me
and I was thinking of her,
and we were both thinking
of that day long ago
when America had asked us

its question,
and we had not known the answer—
And we thought maybe
it had taken a long time
to come to this knowledge . . .

The rain of a San Francisco winter
was warming to the cold
of a San Francisco summer,
a day every young person knows,
when a pulse of corn-flowers
lights up the snow—
Gulls cried over the hill-climbing houses
and a painting of the sea,
and cable-cars screeched
like carnival rides,

and we were there,
knocking on doors,
our ears full of prosody,
looking for the last great
gay bard of these States,
who wrote it all down
in his short-hand poesy
and angelic bop-headed
poetry of dawn . . .

—An African came
to the table before us.

He wore a watch-cap
and army coat.
He sat hands-in-pockets,
silent—
His stare brimmed
with an intensity
that had its own take
on the misfortunes of
middle-class children.

When someone says
I've been an African
a slave a share-cropper
convict horn player
invented singing as a cure
for depression
and a hop-head,
what have you been—?
Sometimes silence
is the only answer you give . . .

He entered in silence,
sat down in silence;
he looked at us in silence,
stood up in silence
and went out again in silence.
His eyes said
don't look for someone else

to help straighten you out—
The coffee-house was emptier
when he left
and a door slammed in the cold.

America, you are not hard
to figure out—
I have been overthinking you.
If you see Jesus with an AK-47,
tell him America is happiness.

Storm clouds over highway ramp,
gas-cloud fumes on freeway,
lights on radio masts
blinking under low clouds,
toll-booth change flying,
scrounging under car frame;

Jersey City drag-queen
on radio calls shaved-ape love-child
with Pope miracle birth,
takes Holy Communion—
Nibiru trumpet,
sound of hell-gate opening.

A horde of shoppers appears,
being flogged through a mall—
They are running hard,

arms full of bags,
breath short in their throats,
no time for the food court.

A herd of cattle being driven
to the slaughter-house floor
would be frightened,
but these people are not frightened.
There's no word to describe
what I see in their eyes.

No day or night here,
only the even over-glow
of an artificial climate,
where no onrush of shopping
can blunt an inexorable logic:
you can't see death but
the people who are trying
to hide should try harder—
Driven on by invisible shocks,
past kiosks of merchants
who learned how to bargain
in Muhammadan souks . . .

The cattle being driven
to the slaughter-house door
long only for the feed-lot
and a trough full of grain,

or to be on a prairie
with a flute of short-grass,
inhaling a scent as from
shale-rock and sunflowers,
and the land like a cloth
on the ground,
billowing as if to invite us . . .

Sit, and be rested—
Sit under the roof
of our kodachrome sky,
blue as a coal-miners eyes,
drawing its majesty
from some as yet unseen
range of mountains
sharpened by snow,

consider the ghosts of
immigrants still passing,
their wheel-ruts scratched
on sagebrush plains;
consider broom-faced men,
pansy-bonneted women,
dusty cherubim leading
drooping oxen,
wagons piled with player pianos
and trousseau chests;

consider every road
is a history of immigrant hordes . . .

The woman beside me was silent,
wrapped in the wind
that sang in her hair,
and her lips moved
with her thoughts
that were like poems,
waiting to be translated into speech—

Woman, where are you?
Do you remember the night
we camped in a cemetery?
You called it a junkyard
of souls and we closed
our eyes among stones
that were lined up like sharks' teeth
and obelisks and broken
columns were thick
as a forest that died
in an ocean of salt,
and woke in the morning
and agreed we had dreamed
of a country
that was trying to kill us.

Where have the children
of Sandy Hook gone?
Where has Trayvon Martin gone?
Where are the dead
of the Boston Marathon?
Where are the dead
of the Taconic Parkway?

Have they all walked away
on the legs
of the Marathon bombing?
I believe one of those
Sandy Hook children
knew the secret of life.
Everyday in this country
someone else climbs
the stages of grief on their knees . . .

We had long ago found America
and America was closed.
America is failure
and its people are death.

We wanted to write America
but no one knew what
America was anymore.
We wanted to write the vernacular
but no one knew

how to speak it anymore.
We wanted to sound the
American theme
but no one knew
what it was anymore . . .

We wanted to see our poems
in the lights of the signs
and words of the billboards
that loomed over streets
and the sides of roads—
We wanted our stories
to be sold in every drug-store
and our books in every
bus-station and airport.
We wanted our veins
to glow with the neon
of the American soul.

Go, friend, return to the dead—
You have been gone
long enough.
I came back for you.
It was too late.

Boundaries

She showed me the fence
where horses pressed,
and the few strands of wire
that held back
their fleet curious heads,

and how they frightened her—
We got to know each other then,
how she loved chai lattes
and didn't like coffee,
and I loved coffee,
and didn't like tea,
and these were our boundaries.

But if the subjunctive
has a reason for existing,
it finds it in imagining,
for only in imagining
can anything happen—

As for me, I am entirely
subjunctive.
I am an amphibian of reality.
I have drifted for eons
with only my eyes above water.

But alas—everything pulls
against a few strands of wire,

like stitches in a wound:
women have eyes only
for professional men.

David Churchill

Waiting for Greatness

"We were raised to be famous."
Kathi Ambrogi, 2017

The summer sun sinks
on the stones in the alley,
sinks on the blooms
of johnny-bean trees
shading the shanty-town
backs of houses,

leaving the sky a worn
gray, too early
for bed but day's end
nonetheless,
and I am ready for sleep,
for I have been
waiting for greatness—
and I am all in . . .

Even now I hear
that lullaby a woman sang
as waves of sleep
rowed us away.
The moon came up
beyond the window,
and night was a journey
two took alone.

Woman, who were you
who sang to me
so long ago,
who began with a lullaby
and became a siren of deception?

These backs of houses
hide a different truth.
No one sings here now.
A dream-man walks
through sleepless worlds,
and night falls
like a handful of dust.

At a picnic I am wearing
a tuxedo.
At a party I am missing
an orchestra.
At a bus-stop
I have no limousine.

Here dwell all
who have no place,
or do not know
where is their place.
The mother of places
has nothing to give,
though she gives what she can . . .

An Occasion of Roses

I thought about you today.
I put down a book
by that Danish philosopher,
and considered how love
is transcendent
because of its timelessness,

and in particular, first love—
Not because it is first in a series,
but because it can never
be repeated again . . .

Do you remember where we met?
A spring rain had fallen
and bushes of baby's
breath floated in buckets,
and roses so soft
they would have crushed
if touched too hard
exhaled around us,
and a fresh-cut scent filled the air.

Now when I look at my face
I remember your eyes,
how everything you saw
improved in their depths,
and I see myself as I was.
I see it so clearly sometimes

I could stand in front
of something shiny all day.

If only we could have been
like a coming breeze
from a month of extremes,
mingling winter cold
and summer heat,
as the young are extreme
and the old depleted—
If we saw each other again,
all we would have lost
would have been a little time.

But better this is all we have,
a little book on philosophy—
How can two people
love each other forever
without turning time back,
unless they find new time . . . ?
And maybe they do.

www.ingramcontent.com/pod-product-compliance
Lightning Source LLC
Chambersburg PA
CBHW021338090426
42742CB00008B/646

* 9 7 8 0 9 7 5 3 0 9 5 5 1 *